KB050681

어원+어원=영단어

김준우

박영사

One Art

Elizabeth Bishop

The art of losing isn't hard to master;
so many things seem filled with the intent
to be lost that their loss is no disaster.

Lose something every day.
Accept the fluster of lost door keys,
the hour badly spent.
The art of losing isn't hard to master.

Then practice losing farther,
losing faster: places, and names,
and where it was you meant to travel.
None of these will bring disaster.

...

--Even losing you (the joking voice, a gesture I love)
I shan't have lied.
It's evident the art of losing's not too hard to master
though it may look like (Write it!) like disaster.

서 문

'어원 + 어원 = 영어 단어' 방식으로 1장이 시작된다. pro(forward) + ject(throw) = project'라는 공식은, 5분 공부를 가능하게 한다. 그림이 많아, 직관적 이해가 쉽다. 재미있는 예문도 많다.

When life hands you a lemon, squeeze it and make lemonade.

If life gives you lemon, squeeze them in people's eyes.

기본 동사 어원에 집중한다. 많이 쓰이는 동사는, 생각보다 중요하다. 그래서 비슷한 동사를 구분하는 2장이 이어진다. ject(throw) 어원을 반복하면서, 동사의 완벽한 이해를 시도한다. cast, hurl과 같은 동사와 다른 점을 설명한다.

'삶 = 언어 표현'이라는 공식이 3장에서 나온다. 서양인의 삶은 영어 표현에 녹아 있다. 당연히 서양의 경험은 동양과 비슷하면서도 또 다르기도 하다.

중학교 영어 수준에서 시작해서, 높은 수준까지 갈 수 있는 책이다. 부록에 담긴 어원 조합은, 꼭 시간 들여 즐기면서 보기를 권한다.

어머니를 위해 기도해주신 최상준 유스티노 신부님과 간병해주신 이무순 이모에게 감사드린다. 부산연구원 금성근, 황영우 박사님과 얘기를 들어주시는 박상훈 선생님에게도 감사드린다. 고마운 고향 친구들이(구진만, 김중모, 박재영, 신현덕, 안준모, 유영준, 정우철, 정유인) 또 있다.

고대 사회학과 박길성 교수님은 뵐 때마다 힘이 되어 주셨다. 뵐 때마다 많이 배우기도 했다. 향상심을 늘 보여주신다.

딸 김단아 에스더 덕분에 친절한 본문과 간결한 제목이 나왔다. 아들 김지환 다윗은 재미있다 얘기해주었다.

오준, 박건우, 문재규, 남철민, 오성현, 김동주, 곽두만, 류미선, 남진구, 도성일, 박창민, 안현우, 유재성, 황인원, 이찬호, 황건호, 강긍원, 나지온, 김상현, 김설, 김정현, 이원필, 임도솔, 노동국, 황소연, 조예은, 노영수, 이성재, 김찬영, 정명원, 최지웅, 김재현, 권소연 학생과의 시간이 바로 이 책이다.

꼼꼼하게 원고를 봐 주신 우석진 선생님, 표지를 만들어 주신 최윤주 선생님, 과정을 진행해 주신 이영조 차장이 손으로 만질 수 있게 책을 만들어 주셨다.

2021년
저자

차 례

서양인의 삶과 영어 표현

어원 더하기 어원

01 공기를 '이끌어 내는' '덕트 duct'

- 덕트 duct = 공기를 어느 곳으로 이끌어 나가는 통로. 환 기통이다. 건물 바깥에서 보면 그림[1])과 같이 보인다.
- duct = 이끌다 lead

- 은색 강력 테이프가 덕트테이프 duct tape
- 그랜 토리노 Gran Torino 영화에 나오는 대사이다.

---

1) https://ac-illust.com/ko/clip-art/229879/

duct tape

Take these three items, some WD-40, a vise grip, and a roll of duct tape. Any man worth his salt can fix almost any problem with this stuff alone.

- 미국 일상 필수품이 나온다. 뿌리는 녹 방지 윤활유 WD-40, 잠금장치가 있는 집게 vise grip.
- 로마 군인은 급여로 소금을 받기도 했다.
  소금 salt. 급여 salary. 군인 soldier.

> **aque(water) + duct(lead) = aqueduct**

- 물을 나르는 통로 = aqueduct [ǽkwədʌkt].[2] 로마 기술 최고봉으로 꼽히는 수로교이다.

> **ab(away) + duct(lead) = abduct**

---

2) https://ac−illust.com/ko/clip−art/242270/

■ 벗어나서 이끌어 나간다 → 납치하다 abduct[əbdʌkt].
명사는 abduction. 동사 명사 모두, 발음 강세가 두 번째
모음에 있다.

If someone attempts to abduct you, make noise.

Issuing an insurance policy against abduction by
aliens seems a pretty safe bet. - Steven Hawking

■ 외계인 유괴에3) 대비한 보험을 파는 것은 남는 장사 deal

[diːl]. insurance policy = 보험증권 (보험 계약 성립을 증명하는 문서).

■ abduction, kidnap[kídnæp] 두 단어는 구분 없이 쓰기도 한다. 우주인이 데리고 가는 경우는, abduct만 사용한다. 왜 데리고 가는지가 분명하지 않기 때문이다.

■ 우주인이 몸값을 요구한다면, kidnap 사용 가능하다.

---

pro(forward) + duce(lead) = produce

■ 앞으로 forward 이끌어 나간다 lead → 생산하다 produce [prədjúːs]

■ 1913년 포드 자동차 대량생산 mass production 장면.[4]

Money has never made man happy, nor will it, there is nothing in its nature to produce happiness. – Benjamin Franklin

The darkest nights produce the brightest stars. – John Green

---

de(down) + duce(lead) = deduce

---

3) https://ac−illust.com/ko/clip−art/1442057/

4) https://upload.wikimedia.org/wikipedia/commons/2/29/Ford_assembly_line_−1913.jpg

- 밑으로 이끌어 가면 deduction이다. 세금공제 tax deduction 역시 과세기준을 밑으로 이끌어 내린다.

When you fall in love, you must fall in love with a man the way he is now, because marriage won't change anything, except maybe your tax deduction.
- Kathie Lee Gifford

- 위에서부터 밑으로 끌어 내리는 논리 → deduction 연역. 상위 대전제에서부터 추론. deduce[didjúːs] 추론하다.

모든 사람은 죽는다.
소크라테스는 사람이다.
소크라테스는 죽는다.

■ your silence가 대전제, do not approve가 추론이다.
Can we deduce from you silence that you do not approve?

---

re(back, again) + duce(lead) = reduce

■ 뒤로 가다 → 작게 만들다 reduce [ridjúːs]

Worries don't motivate us, they reduce our energy and opportunity to shine. - Bamigboye Olurotimi

---

se(apart) + duce(lead) = seduce

■ 떼어내어 이끌어 나간다 → 유혹하다 seduce[sidjúːs]

I find the fragrance to be such a mood enhancer and definitely a seduction tool. - Christina Aguilera

Seduce my mind and you can have my body, find my soul and I'm yours forever. - MD Waters

True love is the love that seduces and will never allow itself to be seduced. - Paulo Coelho

02 '앞으로 pro' '던지는 ject' '프로젝터 projector'

- ject = 던지다. throw 동사에 해당한다.[1]

- 던지는 throw 대상이 사물인 경우가 많다. 하지만 생각을 던진다는 의미로도 꽤나 쓰인다.

> pro(forward) + ject(throw) = project

---

1) やり投げ http://pictogram2.com/

- 앞으로 던지다 → project[prədʒékt]. 동사로 쓰이는 경우는 대체로 이러하다. 예정되거나 예측된다는 의미로서 쓰이고, 또 수동 형태로 나온다.

China's GDP is projected to grow despite COVID-19.

- 이 의미의 명사는 projection[prədʒékʃən].

US economy is not in 'free fall' despite 32% unemployment projection.

- 영상을 앞으로 내던지면, projector[prədʒéktər].[2]

- projectile[prədʒéktil] = 발사체
- 발사체는 중력 지배를 받는 던져진 모든 것이다. 로켓, 화살, 총알, 포탄과 같은 무기가 흔히 연상된다. 유도장치가 있는 미사일도 포함된다. 무기가 아닌 발사체도 있다. 야구공도 발사체이다.

---

2) プロジェクターのアイコン素材 https://icooon-mono.com/

- projectile 표현을 사용하는 경우, 아직 미사일인지 여부가
확인 되지 않았다는 의미이다. 아래 예문에서는 그렇다.

North Korea launched a projectile into the ocean.

- 심리학 투사 projection 개념이다. 생각을 던진다.

Don't project your negative feelings on me!

- project[prάdʒekt] = 해야 할 일. 흔히 우리가 생각하듯,
어떤 공식적 과제만을 의미하지는 않는다.

The more people you have to ask for permission,
the more dangerous a project gets. - Alain de Botton

There are two fatal errors that keep great projects
from coming to life: 1) Not finishing 2) Not starting.
- Buddha

---

in(into) + ject(throw) = inject

- 안으로 in 던져 넣다 ject → 주입하다3). in은 들어가는 과
정을 중요시하는 into 의미이다.

---

3) 犬の予防注射のイラスト https://www.irasutoya.com/2014/03/blog-post_335.html

■ 주사하다 inject[indʒékt]. 손으로 살짝 잡히던 문에 세게 찍히던, 피부에 힘이 작동될 때 pinch[pinʧ]를 쓴다.

Inject the needle into the pinched skin at a 90 degree angle.

Some people believe it is unnatural to inject vaccines into our body.

■ 생각을 넣는다는 의미로도 쓰인다. 건포도 raisin[réizn], 밀가루 반죽 dough[dou] 둘 다 흔한 서양 식재료이다.

Inject a few raisins of conversation into the tasteless dough of existence. - O. Henry

When we inject people with positivity, their outlook expands. They see the big picture. When we inject them with neutrality or negativity, their peripheral vision shrinks. There is no big picture, no dots to connect. - Barbara Fredrickson

---

re(back) + ject(throw) = reject

■ 뒤로 던져진다 thrown back 의미이다.[4] reject[ridʒékt] = 거부하다. 거부 대상에는 사람도 포함된다.

We tend to overvalue the people who reject us.

Most fears of rejection rest on the desire for approval from other people. Don't base your self-esteem on their opinions. - Harvey Mackay

■ conjecture[kəndʒéktʃər] = 추측하다.[5] '생각을 모으다'에서 유래한다.[6] 근거 없이 억측하다는 느낌이 강하다.

---

con(together) + jecture(throw) = conjecture

■ heavy duty 표현은 옷, 기계, 장비에 쓰인다. 튼튼하게 만들어져 거친 환경에도 버틸 수 있다.
■ That's some heavy duty conjecture. = 꽤나 정교한 억측이네요.

---

4) Oxford Languages
5) https://ac−illust.com/ko/clip−art/1741621/
6) https://www.lexico.com/en/definition/conjecture

■ 나이브스 아웃 Knives Out 대사이다. The knives are out. 사람들이 칼을 꺼내 밖으로 내놓았다는 의미이다.

"That's some heavy duty conjecture."
"Granted. But it is the only way of what comes next makes sense. So, you storm out, you drive off into the night. You tell Martha later of, what was it? Feeling an overwhelming sense of …"

■ 아래에서는 그냥 추측한다는 의미이다. 중립적 느낌이다.

The purpose of life is to conjecture and prove. - Paul Erdos

03 '누르는' '프레스 press'

- press = 누르는 기계[1]

- press 포함 세 단어를 살펴보자. oppress, suppress, repress 차이[2]를 알아보자.

---

1) press.png   www.flaticon.com
2) longman wordwise dictionary

---

ob(against) + press = oppress

- 맞서서 ob 눌러대면 press → oppress[əprés]. oppress = 억압하다. 명사 oppression.
- 정부가 주로 누른다. 중국 정부가 소수 민족을 수용소에 가두면, oppress 하는 것이다

The Chinese government is oppressing ethnic religious minorities in Xinjiang, China.

- 억압받는 사람 = the oppressed

Time is on the side of the oppressed today, it's against the oppressor. Truth is on the side of the oppressed today, it's against the oppressor. You don't need anything else. - Malcolm X

- 편 = the side
- I am on your side. = 나는 너 편이다.
- Whose side are you on? = 너는 누구 편이야?
- 로마 역사가 타키투스에 따르면, 억압에 맞서려는 욕구는 인간 본성에 심어져 있다.
- into + 식물을 심다 plant = 사람에 심다 implant

A desire to resist oppression is implanted in the nature of man. - Tacitus

---
sub(under) + press = suppress

- sub → sup
- 밑으로 sup 짓누르면 press → suppress. 정부가 폭력을 사용하면, suppress 동사를 주로 쓴다.
- tear[tiər] gas 최루 가스, rubber bullet 고무탄

Hong Kong police used tear gas and rubber bullets to suppress tens of thousands of people demonstrating against the extradition bill.

- the extradition bill 송환법. extradition[èkstrədíʃən]에서 ex 는 'out of'이다. 법안 bill[bil].
- 송환법은 홍콩인을 중국 법원으로 보내 처벌받을 수 있게 한다.

---
re(again, back) + press = repress

- 눌러서 press 뒤로 re 몰리게 한다. repress[riprés]이다. 누르는 주체는 다양하다. 나 자신도 누를 수 있다. 타인 혹은 정부도 가능하다.
- knit[nit] = 뜨개질하다. 뜨개질을 하듯, 사람을 잇는다.

Repression works only to strengthen and knit the repressed. - John Steinbeck

■ trigger[trígər] = 방아쇠나 기폭장치를 당기다, 촉발하다.
서양인의 삶에서 총의 의미는 지대하다. 소총의 시대로 접
어들면, 총은 자기 방어와 사냥에 쓰는 일상용품이 된다.

Next time some harmless situation triggers you or
someone around you into an intense emotion -
realize it's an attempt at emotional healing.
Realize the danger is no longer there, but don't
suppress the healing of old dangers and old pains.
Allow the pain.
Don't react, but don't repress.
Embrace the pain.
Embrace the pain of others. - Vironika Tugaleva

■ 이 세 단어를 정리해보자.

ob(against) + press = oppress
sub(under) + press = suppress
re(again, back) + press = repress

oppress   누르는 주체는 정부
suppress   누르는 주체는 정부, 폭력 동반
repress   누르는 주체는 정부, 나 자신, 타인

■ 늘 이 도식처럼은 아니다. suppress 주체가 자기 자신이
되기도 한다. 예문을 보자! 자신감정을 폭력적으로 누르면
우울증이 온다.

Suppressing your emotions can lead to depression.

■ 개인도 자신과 관련된 무엇을 폭력적으로 누를 수 있다. 그래서 suppress 사용이 가능하다고 이해해도 무방하다.

As long as you keep secrets and suppress information, you are fundamentally at war with yourself … The critical issue is allowing yourself to know what you know. That takes an enormous amount of courage. - Bessel A. van der Kolk

de(down) + press = depress

■ 아래쪽으로 down 누르다 press → depress[diprés]. 그림[3]은 밑으로 눌러져 있는 마음 상태를 아주 잘 보여준다. 심리용어 depression = 우울증. 경제용어 depression = 불황. Great Depression = 대공황.

Suppressing your emotions can lead to depression.

The Great Depression began with the stock market crash of 1929.

ex(out of) + press = express

3) https://ac−illust.com/ko/clip−art/844658

- 밖으로 ex 눌러 내보내다 press → 표현하다[iksprés]

  Unexpressed emotions will never die. They are buried alive and will come forth later in uglier ways. - Sigmund Freud

- 같이 with 누르면 press, 압축하다 compress[kəmprés][4]

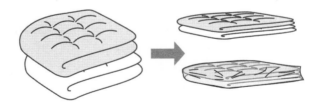

- compressor[kəmprésər] = 압축기
- 비행기 제트 엔진은 공기를 압축기 거쳐 연소실로 보낸다.
- 파일 압축할 때에도 사용한다.

---

4) https://ac-illust.com/ko/clip-art/1247007/

How do I compress files into a zip file?

---

im(into) + press = impress

■ 마음 안쪽으로 들어가게 해서 im 눌러 각인시키다 press → 호감 혹은 존경심을 가지게 하다 impress[imprés]

Thomas wanted to impress his girlfriend, so he polished his best boots.

Don't try to impress people. Always be yourself! - Bella Thorne

■ 인상 = impression. 순간 들어오는 느낌을 그리면, 인상주의 impressionism 작품이다. tread[tred] 발을 땅에 딛다.

A thousand words will not leave so deep an impression as one deed. - Henrik Ibsen

Never tread lightly. Leave a deep impression wherever you go. - K. Rafferty

04 '꼬아서 tor' 괴롭히는 '고문 torture'

■ 몸을 비틀면 tor, 고문 torture [tɔ́ːrtʃər]. 어원 tort 경우
는, 비틀다 twist 의미이다. 그림은 twist hair.[1]

---

1) https://ac-illust.com/ko/clip-art/1955577/

■ 바퀴를 돌리는 힘이 토크 torque [tɔːrk]. 자동차 주요 성
능 중 하나이다.

---

ex(out of) + tort(twist) = extort

■ 남의 몸을 비틀어서 twist 돈을 뜯어내다 밖으로 out of
→ 갈취하다 extort[ikstɔ́ːrt].

The pizzo (Italian: ['pittso]) is protection money paid
to the Mafia often in the form of a forced transfer
of money, resulting in extortion.

---

dis(away) + tort(twist) = distort

■ 엇나가서 away 틀어지게 하다 twist → 비틀리게 하다
distort [distɔ́ːrt]

Don't let other people's opinions distort your reality.
Be true to yourself. Be bold in pursuing your
dreams. - Steve Maraboli

■ 지형이 꼬이면 tor → tortuous[tɔ́ːrtʃuəs]

The Tigris in parts is wonderfully tortuous, and at
one great bend, 'The Devil's Elbow,' a man on foot

can walk the distance in less than an hour which takes the steamer four hours to accomplish. - Isabella Bird

- 바그다드를 끼고 굽어 돌아가는 티그리스 강2)
- bend[bend] 굽은 곳. elbow[élbou] 팔꿈치. devil[dévl] 악마. steamer[stíːmər] 증기선.
- ac<toward> + complish<complete> = accomplish [əkɑ́mpliʃ] 갈 길을 다 가다, 성취하다

- 인생길이 굴곡져도, tortuous 하다.

Life is but a hard and tortuous journey.

- 꼬는 것 tor → 괴로움 torment[tɔ́ːrment]

You may be deceived if you trust too much, but you will live in torment if you don't trust enough. - Frank Crane

---

2) https://en.wikipedia.org/wiki/Tigris#/media/File:Tigris_River_in_Baghdad_(2016).jpg

05 '팽팽해지는 tend' '긴장 tension'

■ tend = 팽팽하게 쭉 펼치다 stretch[1]

■ tension[ténʃən] = 잡아당김, 긴장, 갈등.

Steel is equally strong in tension and compression.
Steel is weak in fires, and must be protected in
most buildings.

---

1) https://ac−illust.com/ko/clip−art/1964671/

■ 마음에 관한 예문도 있다.

Kill tension before tensions kill you, reach your goal before goal kicks you, live life before life leaves you. - Sanam Sri

Maturity is achieved when a person accepts life as full of tension; when he does not torment himself with childish guilt feelings, but avoids tragic adult sins; when he postpones immediate pleasures for the sake of long-term values. - Joshua L. Liebman

■ 여기서 childish[ʧáildiʃ]는 맥락을 보면 알 수 있듯이, 부정적 느낌이다. 긍정적 의미의 childlike[ʧáildlàik]과 다르다.

childish = immature 미성숙한
childlike = innocent 순진무구한

■ tension의 형용사는 tense이다.
■ 근육에 대한 예문이다.

Why are my muscles so tense?

Muscle rigidity is often triggered by stress.

■ 비유적으로는 빡빡하고 긴장감이 흐르는 상황을 의미한다.
■ 영화 조커 Joker 대사이다. 팽팽하게 펼쳐져 언제 끊어질

지 모르는 불안한 상황이다.

Arthur Fleck: Is it just me, or is it getting crazier out there?
Social Worker: It is certainly tense. People are upset, they're struggling, looking for work. These are tough times.

- tend to = ~하는 경향이 있다. 어떠한 쪽으로 쭉 뻗어 나가는 어감을 주는 표현이다. 명사는 tendency[téndənsi].
- 여기서 myth[miθ]는 신화가 아니다. 실제로는 틀린 것인데도 많은 사람이 믿고 있는 생각이다.

Myths which are believed in tend to become true.
- George Orwell

- 망치를 들면, 모든 게 못으로 보이게 된다.

If you only have a hammer, you tend to see every problem as a nail. - Abraham Maslow

- tendon[téndən] = 힘줄. 근육에 붙은 끈이다.2) 어원은 동일하다. 팽팽하게 쭉 펼치다!

---

2) https://ac-illust.com/ko/clip-art/526474/

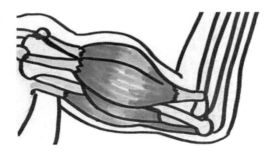

- 팽팽하게 쭉 펼쳐서 stretch 텐트 tent 세운다.[3]

---

at(to) + tend(stretch) = attend

- 어디로 to 뻗다 stretch → 돌보다 attend [əténd]

The doctor will attend to you in a moment.

The tenderness of God is present in the lives of all those who attend the sick and understand their needs, with eyes full of love. - Pope Francis

---

■ attend = ~에 다니다, ~에 참석하다.

To be a doctor, you have to attend medical school.

Attend funerals avoid weddings. - Arabic Proverbs

■ attendant[əténdənt] = 종업원, 안내원, 점원

Most of us have jobs that require some handling of other peoples' feelings and our own, and in that sense, we are all partly flight attendants.
- Arlie Russell Hochschild

---

ex(out) + tend(stretch) = extend

■ 밖으로 out 팽팽하게 쭉 펼치다 stretch → 확장하다 extend [iksténd]. 물리적 그리고 비유적 의미로 쓴다.

Dance is bigger than the physical body. When you extend your arm, it doesn't stop at the end of your fingers, because you're dancing bigger than that; you're dancing spirit. - Judith Jamison

With practice and focus, you can extend yourself far more than you ever believed possible. - Edmund Hillary

---

con(together) + tend(stretch) = contend

- 같이 together 팽팽하게 하다 stretch → ~을 두고 싸우다 contend[kənténd]
- 싸움에서 서로를 당겨 팽팽해지는 느낌을 생각하자!4)

- master[mǽstər]은 종을 거느리는 주인이다.

When people contend for their liberty they seldom get anything for their victory, but new masters. - Edward F. Halifax

- 싸움에서 지다, ~을 잃다 = lose[luːz]

Never contend with someone who has nothing to lose. - Baltasar Gracián

- 개와 고양이가 싸우는 느낌이, contentious[kənténʃəs].

---

4) 柔道 2 http://pictogram2.com/

My dad and I have had contentious relationship ever since I was a young teenager.

- cor<with> + rode<scratch> = corrode[kəróud] 녹슬다
- un<not> + re<back> + lenting<bending> = unrelenting [ə͵nrile'ntiŋ] 끊임없는, 수그러들지 않는
- argument[ɑ́ːrgjumənt] = 말싸움

Our spirits are corroded by living in an atmosphere of unrelenting contention - an argument culture. - Deborah Tannen

- bone of contention[kənténʃən] = 두 마리 개가 서로 물고 잡아당기며 싸우는 뼈다귀.
- for decades 수십 년 동안. decade[dékeid] 십 년.
- 십진법 the decimal[désəməl] system.
- decimate[désəmèit]는 '로마 병사 열 명당 한명씩 골라 처형하다'에서 나왔다. 현재는 많은 이를 죽인다는 의미.

The border between India and China has been a bone of contention for decades.

> **pre(before) + tend(stretch) = pretend**

- 사람 앞에서 before 자신을 쭉 펼치는 stretch 행위가 pretend[priténd].

- 옛날 pretend 의미는, 주장하다 claim[kleim]. 상거래에서 흔히 얘기하는 클레임. 상대방이 계약내용을 충실히 이행하지 않을 경우, 손해배상을 주장하는 것이다.
- 현재는 주장에 거짓이 더해진다.
- pretend = ~가 아닌데도 불구하고 ~인 척하다.

Don't pretend to be someone you are not.

Sometimes I pretend to be normal. But it gets boring. So I go back to being me. - Ain Eineziz

Don't pretend you care when you don't.

It's hard to pretend you love someone when you don't, but it's harder to pretend that you don't love someone when you really do.

Pretending! I am so good at it, you'll never know I am doing it.

06 '중요한 important' '항구 port'

■ 항구 port[1]는 예나 지금이나 중요하다.

---

1) https://ac-illust.com/ko/clip-art/1144698/

- port에서 짐을 나르는 사람이 짐꾼 porter[pɔ́ːrtər]. 여기서 나르다 carry 의미가 나온다.
- Porter은 직업에서 나온 이름이다. 이런 이름을 더 알아보자! Archer, Baker, Carter, Fisher, Hunter, Judge, Mason, Parker, Potter, Smith, Taylor, Thatcher
- 수입하다 import[impɔ́ːrt]는 항구 안으로 무언가를 들여오는 것이다. 수출하다 export[ikspɔ́ːrt]는 항구 밖으로 무엇인가를 내보내는 것이다. 명사는 발음이 달라진다. 수입 = import[ímpɔːrt], 수출 export[ékspɔːrt]

---

im(into) + port(carry) = import

Even desert city Dubai imports its sand. Desert sand is too smooth to be used in construction. - Renuka Rayasam 6th May 2016 BBC

They import and consume reality. - Robinson Jeffers

---

ex(out of) + port(carry) = export

Laughter is America's most important export. - Walt Disney

One does not export democracy in an armored vehicle. - Jacques Chirac

- 항구로 들어오는 물건은 중요하다.
- 수입하다 import → 중요하다 important[impɔ́ːrtənt]
- 명사 import[ímpɔːrt] = 명사 importance
- 옛 영어 명사 import는, 의미나 취지와 연결된 느낌이다.

It is easier to discover a deficiency in individuals, in states, and in Providence, than to see their real import and value. - Georg Wilhelm Friedrich Hegel

- 너머로 across + 나르다 carry = 운송하다[trænspɔ́ːrt]
- 명사는 transport [trǽnsport].

> **trans(across) + port(carry) = transport**

Success is a journey. The best form of transport is Happiness. - Roy Smoothe

Travel is a new experience that can transport you out of your everyday routine to create memories with the ones you love. - Brian Chesky

> **re(again, back) + port(carry) = report**

- 다시 나르다 → 보고하다 report[ripɔ́ːrt]. 명사 보고서 역시 철자와 발음이 동일하다.
- 장문이라서 by its very length, 읽히는 위험 the risk of

being read, 막아내는 defend, 이 보고서 this report.

This report, by its very length, defends itself against
the risk of being read. - Winston Churchill

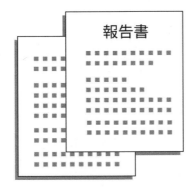

- sub(under) + port(carry) 공식에서 벗어나, 다른 가설을
  보자! suffer patiently → support[səpɔ́ːrt]
- '참을성 있게 견디다 suffer patiently'에서[2] '도움 주다,
  보호 해주다'로, 또 이후에 '비용을 감당하다'로 변화한다.
- 20세기에는 '운영을 가능하게 하다' 의미가 추가된다. 예
  로 tech support[3]가 있다.
- 현재는 도덕적 지지 느낌이 두드러진다.[4]

> **pur(< pro = forward) + port(carry) = purport**

2) https://www.etymonline.com/word/support
3) https://ac-illust.com/ko/clip-art/108877/
4) https://ac-illust.com/ko/clip-art/2003802

- 이제 주로 동사로 사용되는 purport[pərpɔ́ːrt]를 보자.
- 앞으로 pur 나르다 carry 둘이 합쳐진 purport 원래 뜻은 의도하다.
- ~라는 취지를 의도하다는 법률 용어로의 활용이, 나쁜 어감을 가져온다. 법정에서의 의도는 거짓으로 드러나는 경우가 많기 때문이다.
- purport = ~라고 거짓으로 주장하다.

No one is ever who they purport to be. - Cate Blanchett.

- purport 동사가 중립적으로 쓰이기도 한다.
- 확인되지 않았지만 진실일 수도 있는 내용을 주장하다 정도의 느낌이다.
- 예를 들어, 중국 싼샤(三峽) 댐 붕괴 가능성은 진실일 수 있다.[5]

A Twitter user posted recent satellite photos from Google Maps last week purporting to show the Three Gorges Dam had bent and was at risk of breaking.

- Three Gorges가 싼샤 혹은 삼협 三峽 이다.
- gorge[gɔːrdʒ] = 협곡 峽 [xiá]
- 굽다 동사의 시제 변화는 bend-bent-bent
- purport[pə́ːrpɔːrt]는 명사형이다. 성취하겠다고 알리는 무엇이다. 목적을 의미하는 purpose[pə́ːrpəs]로 대체 가능하다.

Christ illustrates the purport of life as He descends from His transfiguration to toil, and goes forward to exchange that robe of heavenly brightness for the crown of thorns. - Edwin Hubbell Chapin

Freedom is the one purport, wisely aimed at, or unwisely, of all man's struggles, toilings and sufferings, in this earth. - Thomas Carlyle

---

5) www.dailymail.co.uk 9 July 2019. China insists massive Three Gorges Dam is safe after satellite images show the 'distorted' structure is at risk of collapse

07 '때리다 batter' '전투하다 battle'

- 첫째 그림은 아시리아 공성 무기 battering ram.[6]
- batter[bǽtər] = 빠르고, 반복적, 폭력적으로 부딪치다.
- 둘째 그림을 보자! 성벽을 공격하는 나무 막대기 끝 부딪치는 부분이 숫양 머리 모양이다.[7] ram[ræm] = 숫양.
- 경찰이 문 부수는 도구가 battering ram. 양 손으로 잡고서는 사용한다. 커다랗고 기다란 원통형 막대기이다.
- 아쉽게도 현대 battering ram 실물에서는 문과 부딪치는 부분에 숫양 머리 장식이 없다.
- ram 역시 동사로도 쓰인다. 자동차로 의도적으로 충돌할 때 사용한다. Ram it! = 들이 박아버려!

---

6) https://commons.wikimedia.org/wiki/File:Assyrian_siege_of_a_city,_showing_use_of_battering-ram.png
7) https://upload.wikimedia.org/wikipedia/commons/3/3e/0869-Attack-on-the-walls-of-a-besieged-town-q75-500x412.jpg

SIEGE OF A CITY, SHOWING USE OF BATTERING-RAM. (From Nimrud.)

One likes people much better when they're battered down by a prodigious siege of misfortune than when they triumph. - Virginia Woolf

■ 잘 나갈 때보다 얻어터질 때, 사람들은 너를 더 좋아한다.

■ triumph[tráiəmf] 승리. prodigious[prədídʒəs] 엄청난. misfortune[misfɔ́ːrtʃən] 불운. siege[siːdʒ] 포위.

- batter 명사형 battery[bǽtəri] = 폭행. 고의로 힘을 가해서 접촉이 일어나는 경우이다.
- batter[bǽtər] = 빵을 만드는 반죽. 밀가루 설탕 우유를 치고 흔들어서 나오기 때문에 이런 이름이 붙는다.
- 에르도안 집권 이후, 터키 언론이 계속 얻어맞고 있다.8)

In fact, freedom of speech is taking a battering here. In the wake of the failed coup, newspapers have been shut down.

- 날씨 예보에서 batter 동사 사용이 가장 흔하다. 바람, 비, 파도가 어디를 강하고 빠르고 반복적으로 때릴 때 쓴다.

Record-breaking winds and heavy rain batter the UK.

---
com(together) + bat(batter) = combat

- 서로 같이 together 때리다 batter → 교전하다 combat
- combat[kəmbǽt, kάmbæt] 상황에서는 격렬하게 총알과 포탄이 날아다닌다. 조금 다른 단어가 battle[bǽtl].
- 교전 combat 포함하는 것이 전투 battle. 전투에서는 교전 뿐 아니라 여러 상황이 있다. 정찰이나 후퇴도 있다.

---
8) Turkey with Simon Reeve, Series 1, Gallipoli to the Syrian, www.bbc.co.uk

de(< dis = away) + bate(batter) = debate

- 때림에서 battter 벗어나다 away → 토론하다 debate
- 동사도 명사도 debate[dibéit]
- chamber[ʧéimbər] 방. chamber music 실내악.

Freedom means the right of people to assemble, organize, and debate openly. - Hillary Clinton

Debate is healthy and no one in this chamber - starting with me - has a monopoly on being right. - Ted Kulongoski

- beat[biːt] = ~을 막대기로 치다. batter과는 좀 다른 느낌.
- 새 사냥에서 수풀을 막대기로 치고 다니는 것에서 유래한다. 새가 날아오르면, 사냥이 본격화된다.
- beat the bushes = 공을 들여 철저하게 찾아보다

The police are beating the bushes for the suspect, but so far he is nowhere to be found.

He beat the bushes and another caught the birds. - French Proverbs

Beat the bushes for your will in everything you do. - Adarsh Pandey

- beat = 이기다. You beat me! (토론에서) 네가 이겼어!
- beat = 이기다. 스포츠에서 쓰인다. 1 대 0 점수는 one to nothing. 줄여서는 one nothing, 혹은 one nil. one zero 식으로는 읽지 않는다.

Manchester beat Liverpool 1-0.

- beat = 이기다. 바이러스를 이기는 경우에도 사용한다.[9]

Testing is key to beating coronavirus, right? Japan has other ideas.

- beat = 이기다. 사람을 이기는 경우에도 쓴다.

You just can't beat the person who never gives up.
- Babe Ruth

- beat = 때리다. 너무 자신을 때리지 마! 자책하지 마!

Don't beat yourself up. It's not your fault.

---

9) Ben Dooley and Makiko Inoue, Published May 29, 2020 New York Times

08 '만지다 tact' '접촉하다 contact'

- ~tact = 만지다 touch[1]

- 같이 con 만지면 touch → 접촉하다 contact[kɑ́ntækt][2]

con(together) + tact(touch) = contact

---

1) https://ac-illust.com/ko/clip-art/2066127
2) https://ac-illust.com/ko/clip-art/2053932/

- food = ~할 거리. Some books are full of food for thought! 생각을 하게 하는 책이 있어!

Every mind needs friendly contact with other minds, for food of expansion and growth. - Napoleon Hill

Physical contact is a human necessity. - David Byrne

- 어원 tact는 '민감한 정신적 만지기'라는 뜻도 있다. '물리적 만지기'에서 파생된 것이다.
- 명사 tact도 존재한다. tact[tækt] = 재치, 눈치, 기지.

Tact is the art of making a point without making an enemy. - Isaac Newton

- 지옥으로 꺼지라 얘기하고는, 그 사람이 실제 그 지옥행을 원하도록 만드는 것이 tact이다.

Tact is the ability to tell someone to go to hell in such a way that they look forward to the trip. - Winston Churchill

■ 명사 tact 이외에도, 명사 tactfulness가 있다. 형용사는 tactful[tǽktfəl]이다.

Balance honesty with tactfulness.

■ '물리적 만지기' 혹은 '정신적 만지기'에 당하지 않고 온전한 상태를 intact[intǽkt]라고 한다.

> **in(not) + tact(touched) = intact**

In the practical art of war, the best thing of all is to take the enemy's country whole and intact; to shatter and destroy it is not so good. - Sun Tzu

Change your opinions, keep to your principles; change your leaves, keep intact your roots. - Victor Hugo

Slavery ended and left its false images of black people intact. - John Hendrik Clarke

09 '매달려 있는 pend' '추 pendulum'

- pend = 매달려 있다 hang.
- pendulum[péndʒuləm] = 매달려 흔들리는 추, 진자

Life is like a pendulum: the deeper the sorrow, the more colorful the joy. - Isadora Duncan.

- tyranny[tírəni] 폭정. oscillate[ɔ́silèit] 두 지점을 규칙적으로 오가다. rejuvenate[ridʒúːvənèit] = again + young

- 53 -

The pendulum of the mind oscillates between sense and nonsense, not between right and wrong. - Carl Gustav Jung

Politics is a pendulum whose swings between anarchy and tyranny are fueled by perennially rejuvenated illusions. - Albert Einstein

- anarchy[ǽnərki] = an<without> + archy<leader>.
- per<through> + '한 해의 annual[ǽnjuəl]' = 반복되는
- 소장 아래 매달려 있는 pend 장기가, 맹장 혹은 충수 蟲垂. appendix [əpéndiks][3)]
- 맹장염 appendicitis[əpèndəsáitis]. navel[néivəl] 배꼽. abdomen[ǽbdəmən] 복부.

Appendicitis causes pain in your lower right abdomen. However, in most people, pain begins around the navel and then moves.

- 책 부록도 appendix이며, 매달린 건 다 appendix이다.

A man's life is an appendix to his heart.

---

3) https://ac−illust.com/ko/clip−art/847369

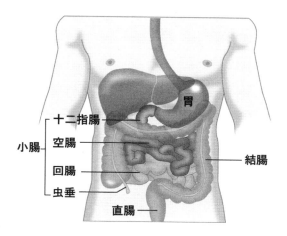

■ 자동차 바퀴가 차체 밑에 under 매달려 있으면 pend →
서스펜션 suspension

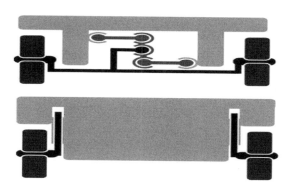

■ suspend[səspénd] = 매달려 있다, 보류되어 있다.
■ 줄에 매달린 다리는 현수교 suspension bridge.
■ 업무에서 배제되어 보류된 상태로 있기도 한다.

sus(under) + pend(hang) = suspend

The police officer was suspended immediately after the shooting.

- suspense[səspéns] = 불안

Even cowards can endure hardship; only the brave can endure suspense. - Mignon McLaughlin

- 서스펜스 영화'4)는 범인이 누군지 잘 알려주지 않는다. suspense = 지속적 긴장상태.

---

4) https://ac−illust.com/ko/clip−art/240520/

> de(down) + pend(hang) = depend

- 밑에 de 매달리다 pend → 의존하다 depend[dipénd]
- 술 끊기 어려워도, depend on 표현이 나온다.5)

Don't depend on others. Do it yourself!

True happiness is ⋯ to enjoy the present, without anxious dependence upon the future. - Lucius Seneca

I never realized how many people in my town depend on alcohol until I started working in a shop that sells it.

---

5) https://ac−illust.com/ko/clip−art/1120928/

- 매달리는 것으로 pending 들어가는 into → 곧 일어나는 impending[impéndiŋ]

> **im(into) + pending(hanging) = impending**

Ignorance of impending evil is far better than a knowledge of its approach. - Cicero

- forbid[fərbíd] 금지하다, 용납하지 않다.
- God forbid = I hope this does not happen.[6]

When a misfortune is impending, I cry, god forbid; but when it falls upon me, I say, god be praised. - Lawrence Sterne

---

6) https://dictionary.cambridge.org/

10 물건을 '같이 con' '잡고 있는 tain' '컨테이너 container'

- tain = 손으로 잡고 있다 hold
- Hold on to it! = 잊어버리지 말고 손으로 잘 잡고 있어!
- Hold your tongue! 혀 tongue[tʌŋ] 손으로 잘 잡고 있어! 함부로 입 놀리지 마!

con(together) + tain(hold) = contain

- 같이 con 잡고 있다 tain → contain[kəntéin]
- contain = 가지고 있다, 포함하다, 함유하다, 억제하다.
- contain = 억제하다. lid 뚜껑. pop off 터져 분리되다.

I try to contain my craziness, but the lid keeps popping off.

- contain = 가지고 있다

Almost all our desires, when examined, contain something too shameful to reveal. - Victor Hugo

■ contain = 포함하다. dull[dʌl] 무디다, 지루하다.

History books that contain no lies are extremely dull. - Anatole France

■ 같이 con 잡고 있는 tain → 컨테이너 container[1]

■ entertain[èntərtéin]은 손 맞잡는 느낌이다.[2]
■ 손잡고 즐거운 시간을 보낸다.

enter(among) + tain(hold) = entertain

■ 여기서 enter이 왜 among의 뜻을 가질까? 프랑스어 entre[ɑ̃tʀ]는 '~사이에'라는 의미이다.

---

1) https://ac-illust.com/ko/clip-art/1614309/
2) https://ac-illust.com/ko/clip-art/280882

■ 손님을 즐겁게 해주는 그러한 느낌이 entertain.

Don't talk to me because you're bored. I'm not here to entertain you. And don't come to me only when you need a favor. I don't like being used. - Ain Eineziz

---

at(to) + tain(hold) = attain

■ 어디로 향해서 to 잡으면 hold → 도달하다 attain[ətéin]
■ 한데 확보하다로 이해하는 것이 더 나은 경우가 있다.
■ 어느 정도의 속도를 확보하는 attain 경우이다. 주로 비행기가 등장한다.

The aircraft reached cruise altitude 22 minutes after departure and attained its target speed of 280 knots.

- 도달하다 느낌을 그대로 구현하는 경우도 물론 있다.
- 성공에 도달하지 attain 못한 예레미야 이야기이다.[3]

WHAT is success? Most definitions include references to achieving goals and acquiring wealth, prestige, favor, and power. "Successful" people enjoy the good life - being financially and emotionally secure being surrounded by admirers, and enjoying the fruits of their labors ... By these standards, Jeremiah was a miserable failure. For 40 years he served as God's spokesman to Judah; but when Jeremiah spoke, nobody listened. Consistently and passionately he urged them to act, but nobody moved. And he certainly did not attain material success.

- attain = 도달하다.
- prompt[prampt] 촉발하다, 신속한. Thank you for your prompt response! 신속한 답변에 감사드립니다!
- stir[stəːr] 젓다, 자극하다. She stirred her tea.

A thought can prompt. Words can stir. But it takes action to attain a dream. - Richelle E. Goodrich

- 추구하다 seek[siːk]-sought-sought[sɔːt]
- ardor[áːrdər] 형용사는 arduous[aːrdʒuəs]. 북한 1990 년대 중후반 식량난 = 고난의 행군 = the arduous march

---

3) Life Application Bible. 1991. Tyndale House Publishers. 1283쪽

Learning is not attained by chance; it must be sought for with ardor and attended to with diligence.
- Abigail Adams

---

de(down) + tain(hold) = detain

- 아래 방향으로 de 잡고 있으면 tain → detain[ditéin] 억류하다 구금하다. 강제로 잡고 있는 것이다.
- Moses[móuziz] 모세. Latino[lətíːnou] (미국에 거주하는) 라틴아메리카계 시민. requisite[rékwəzit] 필요한.
- 동사 배열이 재미있다. 밖으로 나가다 go out, 체포하다 arrest, 구금하다 detain, 추방하다 deport 순이다.

Are we going to go out and arrest and detain and deport 11 million people? Nobody would argue that that is what we are going to do, because we have never demonstrated the political will to do that, nor have we ever committed the requisite resources to do that.

---

sus(under) + tain(hold) = sustain

- 밑에서 sus 근근이 잡다 tain → sustain[səstéin] 한동안 살아있다, 지속하다, 유지하다.
- sustainability [səstèinəbílət i] = 지속가능성

What is the only planet that can sustain life?
Earth!

How can we sustain our natural environment?
Reuse! Recycle!

All philosophy lies in two words, sustain and
abstain. - epictetus

> **abs(away from) + tain(hold) = abstain**

- 잡는 것 tain 으로부터 벗어나 abs → 자제하다 abstain
- (성적 욕구를) 자제하다 = abstain[æbstéin]

Abstaining is favorable both to the head and the
pocket. - W. C. Fields

Virtue consists, not in abstaining from vice, but in
not desiring it. - George Bernard Shaw

- ob 부분의 이해가 까다로운 obtain[əbtéin]
- ob = against 가설보다 나은 건? ~로 향하여 toward!

> **ob(toward) + tain(hold) = obtain**

- 어디로 향해 가다가 손에 잡았다는 느낌이 된다.

- obtain[əbtéin] = 얻다, 입수하다, 취득하다, 획득하다
- 어디로 향해 가다가 명성 fame[feim]을 손에 잡는다. deserve[dizə́ːrv] ~을 받을 만하다, ~을 가질 만하다.

Some people obtain fame, others deserve it. - Doris Lessing

We must not only obtain wisdom: we must enjoy her. - Marcus Tullius Cicero

- 손으로 잡다 tain 어원을 공유하는 또 하나의 단어는 rein[rein]. 손으로 잡는 tain 말 '고삐 rein'이다. 프랑스어로는 rêne[ʀɛn].4)
- give free rein, give full rein = 하고 싶은 대로 할 수 있게 해주다

---

4) https://ac-illust.com/ko/clip-art/735939

- give a ride = 태워주다

  Cowboy wisdom: Never give the devil a ride. He will always want the reins. - unknown

- imagine[imǽdʒin] 상상하다. imagining = imagination.

  Darkness gives free rein to the mind's worst imaginings. - Jocelyn Murray

- 밖에 ex<out> + 쌓다 aggerate<pile up> = 과장하다

  Don't exaggerate. Just give your natural bitchy selves full rein. - Steig Larsson

11 '다시 re' '일어서면 sist' '저항하다 resist'

---

re(against) + sist(stand) = resist

- 맞서서 re 일어서다 sist → 저항하다 resist[rizíst]

It is easier to resist at the beginning than at the end. - Leonardo da Vinci

I can resist everything except temptation. - Oscar Wilde

Resist your fear; fear will never lead to you a positive end. Go for your faith and what you believe. - T. D. Jakes

- 명사는 resistance[rizístəns]
- 불에 저항하는 성질 = fire resistance = 내화성1)

---

per(through) + sist(stand) = persist

- persist[pərsíst] = 어려움이나 반대에도 계속하다
- You are a persistent bastard! = 넌 끈질긴 놈이야!
  영화에서나 나오는 문장이다. 의외로 긍정적 느낌이다.
  persistent[pərsístənt], persistence[pərsístəns].

To be the best, persist during the worst.

The art of love is largely the art of persistence. -
Albert Ellis

Success is about persistence. You can only afford
to be persistent in something you deeply enjoy. -
Cenk Uygur

- 물론 늘 좋은 어감은 아니다. persist = 계속 존재하다.

---

1) https://ac−illust.com/ko/clip−art/803962/

What you resist, persists. - Karl Gustav Jung

It is more honorable to repair a wrong than to persist in it. - Thomas Jefferson

- insist[insíst] = 거절에도 불구하고 계속 주장하다
- 상대방이 선물 받기를 거절하는데도, 계속 받으라는 경우.

Please take it! I insist!

- 부정적 느낌도 많다. 부정적 평가, 거절에도 불구하고 계속 무엇을 주장하기 때문이다. 명사 insistence[insístəns]

Those who insist on the dignity of their office show they have not deserved it. - Baltasar Gracian

- 어느 방향으로 as 일어서다 sist → 돕다 assist[əsíst]. 명사 assistance[əsístəns].

> **as(to) + sist(stand) = assist**

- the fallen 실패한 사람, 전장에서 사망한 병사.

It is a kingly act to assist the fallen. - Mother Teresa

Never look down on anybody unless you're helping

him up. - Jesse Jackson

Give assistance, not advice, in a crisis. - Aesop

---

con(together) + sist(stand) = consist

- 같이 con 일어서다 sist → 구성하다 consist[kənsíst]
- consist of = ~로 구성되다. 물 = 산소 하나 + 수소 둘[2]

Water consists of one oxygen atom and two hydrogen atoms.

- consist in ~에 (본질이) 존재하다, (본질적으로) ~이다. 행복은, 주고 섬기는 것이다. 새 옷이 우아함은 아니다.

Happiness consists in giving and serving others. - Henry Drummond

---

2) https://ac-illust.com/ko/clip-art/739833/

Elegance does not consist in putting on a new dress. - Coco Chanel

Dignity does not consist in possessing honors, but in deserving them. - Aristotle.

■ 밑 under에 서 있다 sist → 근근이 살아가다[səbsíst]

sub(under) + sist(stand) = subsist

■ 생리적으로나 경제적으로, 근근이 살아가는 것이다.
■ chronic[kránik] 만성적.
■ chrono<time> + meter<measure> = 정밀시계 chronometer [krənámətər]

Some chronic severe alcoholics subsist solely on beer.

To blame the poor for subsisting on welfare has no justice unless we are also willing to judge every rich member of society by how productive he or she is. - Norman Mailer

12 '힘 있는 powerful' '힘 있는 potent'

potent = powerful
posse = powerful

- 둘다 힘 있는 powerful 강한 strong 의미이다.

The most potent weapon of the oppressor is the mind of the oppressed. - Steven Biko

- potent[póutnt] = 약효가 센. 명사는 potency [póutnsi].

A highly potent drug evokes a given response at low concentrations. Higher potency does not necessarily mean more side effects.

The experimental coronavirus drug is very potent.

- 어원 posse → 가능하다 possible[pάsəbl]

Start by doing what's necessary; then do what's possible; and suddenly you are doing the impossible. - Francis of Assisi

Politics is the art of the possible, the attainable - the art of the next best. - Otto von Bismarck

- 어원 posse → 소유하다 possess[pəzés]

To have another language is to possess a second soul. - Charlemagne

---

im(not) + potent(powerful) = impotent

- impotence[ímpətəns] 발기부전, hazard[hǽzərd] 위험.

Impotence is one of the major hazards of cigarette smoking. - Loni Anderson

- 달리 무기력한 impotent[ímpətənt] 그런 상태도 있다.[1]

The worst pain a man can have is to know much and be impotent to act. - Herodotus

---

[1] https://ac-illust.com/ko/clip-art/2065830/

Intolerance is evidence of impotence. - Aleister Crowley

- omnipotent[amnípətənt] = 전능한

omni(all) + potent(powerful) = omnipotent

Loneliness is such an omnipotent and painful threat to many persons that they have little conception of the positive values of solitude and even, at times, are frightened at the prospect of being alone. - Rollo May

If God is omnipotent, omniscient and wholly good, whence evil? If God wills to prevent evil but cannot, then He is not omnipotent. If He can prevent evil but does not, then he is not good. In either case he is not God. - David Hume

같은 듯 다른 단어

13 press, crush, squeeze, crumble

- press = 누르는 기계. orange press 오렌지를 눌러 짜내는 기계. printing press 인쇄기.
- 정말 새로워야 hot off the press. 윤전기에서 막 나온 것처럼 뜨거워야 한다. off는 분리를 의미한다.

THE BELLE SAUVAGE MACHINE.   MESSRS. PETTER AND GALPIN

- news hot off the press = 속보 breaking news

Here's some news hot off the press.

Our hot off the press design is now available!

- 윤전기의 누르는 작동에서 언론 표현도 나온다. the press = 언론. 미국에서는 단수 사용을 선호한다.[1]

Freedom of the press is not just important to democracy, it is democracy. - Walter Cronkite

- 누르는 힘 = pressure[préʃər]. 압력솥[2]pressure cooker
- work under pressure = (시간 부족, 여건 열악 등으로) 압박을 받으며 일하다

Must be willing to work under pressure!

- 힘 가해 부수면 crush[krʌʃ].

1) 콜린스 어법사전. Harper Collins 편저. 김방이 편역. 넥서스.
2) https://silhouette−ac.com/ko/silhouette/155317/

- 누르다 + 부서지다 = crush
- 알루미늄 캔을 찌그러뜨리는 느낌이 crush.3)

Anxiety, pressure, and stress can crush us.

Crushed dreams can cause more pain than a broken heart. - Tabitaa Thomas

- 힘을 주어서 쥐어짜는 느낌이 squeeze[skwiːz]이다.4)

---

3) https://silhouette−ac.com/ko/silhouette/176067/
4) https://ac−illust.com/ko/clip−art/647813/

When life hands you a lemon, squeeze it and make lemonade. - Clemont Stone

If life gives you lemon, squeeze them in people's eyes.

■ 빵이나 과자를 손으로 부수면 crumble[krΛmbl].

I always wanted to appear strong and in control … Then the cookie began to crumble. - Chris Evert

I know I would crumble if I lost you. - Shannon

Hale

This world is made out of sugar. It can crumble so easily but don't be afraid to stick your tongue out and taste it. - Sarah Kay

Corfe Castle.

- 건물이나 경제가 무너질 때도 crumble 사용.

Colors fade, temples crumble, empires fall, but wise words endure. - Edward Thorndike

Chinese economy is crumbling due to trade fight.

14 throw, cast, toss, hurl

- throw = 힘을 주어서 던져 무엇을 다른 곳으로 옮기다
- cast[kæst] = 밑으로 던지다.
- The die is cast! = 주사위는 (아래쪽으로) 던져졌다!
- cast = 빛이 아래쪽으로 던져지다

The brightest flame casts the darkest shadow.

All sins cast long shadows. - English Proverbs

■ cast = 그물을 (아래로) 던지다

As Jesus walked beside the Sea of Galilee, he saw Simon and his brother Andrew casting a net into the lake, for they were fishermen. - John 21, 16

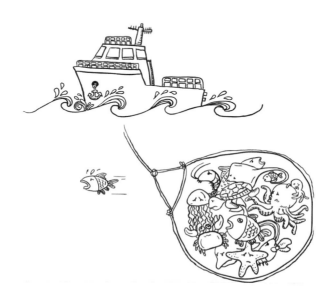

- cast = 표 던지다, 투표하다

- a <without> + pathy <feeling> = apathy. 무관심

If we don't use our right to vote, the country heads for apathy. Get out there and cast your vote.

---

cast(throw) + away(away) = castaway

- 배가 난파되어 표류하다 섬에 도착한 사람 = castaway
- 동사구로서 cast away = 던져서 벗어나게 버려버리다
- 악마 Satan[séitn]. 닻 anchor[ǽŋkər].

We must not lose hope. Hope is an anchor to the souls of men. Satan would have us cast away that anchor. - Ezra Taft Benson

- cast = 뜨거운 액체를 아래로 붓다
- cavus 비다 → 빈 공간 cavity[kǽvəti], 동굴 cave[keiv].
- 이빨 안 빈 공간인 충치는 복수형 사용. dental cavities.
- mold[mould] 틀, 거푸집. 금속 제품은 두 가지 방식으로 만든다. 거푸집에 부어서 뜨는 주물 casting 방식이 있다. 두드려서 만드는 단조 forging[fɔ́ːrdʒiŋ]도 있다.

Casting is the act of pouring liquid material into the cavity of a mold.

If everyone were cast in the same mould, there would be no such thing as beauty. - Charles Darwin

---

fore(before) + cast(throw) = forecast

■ 배 앞부분 fore → before. forecast = 예측하다.

The most reliable way to forecast the future is to try to understand the present. - John Naisbitt

broad(wide) + cast(throw) = broadcast

■ 널리 wide 던지면 throw → 방송하다 broadcast

Broadcasting is really too important to be left to the broadcasters. - Tony Benn

■ 살짝 던지면 toss[tɔːs]. 배구 toss 느낌. 별 신경 안 쓰고 던져서 두는 느낌도 있다. 뒤척이다 = toss and turn

You are the person who has to decide. Whether you'll do it or toss it aside. - Edgar Guest

There's nothing I hate more than nothing. I toss and turn over nothing. - Edie Brickell

■ toss a coin = 동전을 던지다[5]

When faced with two choices, simply toss a coin. It works not because it settles the question for

---

5) https://ac−illust.com/ko/clip−art/2315283

you, but because in that brief moment when the coin is in the air, you suddenly know what you are hoping for.

- hurl[həːrl] = 화나서 폭력적으로 던지다
- hurl stones 대신 threw stones angrily 투입이 가능.

Ukrainians hurl stones at evacuees from China.

Sometimes being a friend means mastering the art of timing. There is a time for silence. A time to let go and allow people to hurl themselves into their own destiny. And a time to prepare to pick up the pieces when it's all over. - Octavia E. Butler

15 twist, spin

- tort = 비틀다 twist
- 몸을 꼬아 괴롭히면, 고문 torture[tɔ́ːrʧər].
- twist는 양 끝을 잡고 힘을 주어서 반대 방향으로 트는 느 낌이다. 앞서 머리를 땋은 그림이 이를 잘 보여준다.
- 트위스트 빵 twist bread 역시 마찬가지이다[1].

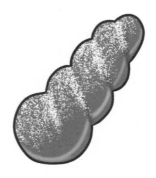

---

1) https://ac－illust.com/ko/clip－art/1825736/

- 인생 비틀림 twist 의미하기도.

Every twist and turn in life is an opportunity to learn something new about yourself, your interests, your talents, and how to set and then achieve goals. - Jameela Jamil

- twist = 새로움
- 고전적 취향 classic taste 그리고 예상하지 못한 새로운 방식 twist, 두 가지가 대조된다.

I have a classic taste with a twist, because classic never goes away. - Nadia Comaneci

- twist = 비틀다.[2] spine[spain] 척추.

---

2) https://ac-illust.com/ko/clip-art/2016270/

Twisting is great for your spine, and it feels good, too.

■ twist = 삐다. ankle[ǽŋkl] 발목. hurt[həːrt] 아프다.

I twisted my ankle and it hurts when I walk.

■ twist someone's arm = 강요하다

Prayer is not trying to twist God's arm to make Him do something. - Andrew Wommack

■ twisted mind = 심각하게 삐뚤어진 마음.
■ cripple[krípl] 장애를 가진. scar[skaːr] 흉터.

Many of the twisted minds and crippled characters in the world were made by careless parents who kept their children away from knives and fires, but put permanent scars on their souls. - Gilbert Highet

■ 두 다른 방향 회전은 twist, 한 방향은 spin[spin].
■ 피겨 스케이트 회전과 지구의 회전, 다 한 방향.

After a few rotations, the skater pulls both arm in closer to the body and spins faster.

The Earth never ceases to spin. All life is dancing : The trees, the wind, the sea. Keep dancing for the rest of your life. - Daisaku Ikeda

■ spin = 어지럽다

My head is spinning, I need to sit on a bed

■ spin = 한 방향 회전을 주다

As the pitcher releases the ball, he snaps his wrist over the ball, putting immense amounts of spin on it.

■ 세상일에도 spin 가능하다.

I try to put a positive spin on things. - Krysten Ritter

■ political spin = 정치인이 먹이는 회전. 이 중 하나가 burying. bury[béri] ~을 땅에 파묻다. 지지율이 떨어뜨리는 사건은, 긴 주말 바로 직전에 발표한다.[3]

Spin may include "burying" potentially negative new information by releasing it at the end of the workday on the last day before a long weekend.

---

[3] Anne Gearan and Yasmeen Abutaleb June 27, 2020 The Washington Post

Pence tries to put positive spin on pandemic despite surging cases in South and West.

- spin off = 분사하다.[4] spinoff, spin-off = 분사 分社
- spin-spun- spun[spʌn]
- diagnostics[dàiəgnástiks] = 진단법(컴퓨터를 활용한)
- dia = through, throughout, across
- dia + gnosis<know> = 진단 diagnosis[dàiəgnóusis]
- dia + logue<speak> = 대화 dialogue[dáiələ̀g]
- dia + meter<measure> = 지름 diameter[daiǽmətər]
- 플로리다 = FL = Fla = Florida

Spin-offs are divisions of companies or organizations that then become independent businesses with assets, employees, intellectual property, technology, or existing products that are taken from the parent company.

Rennova Health plans to spin off its diagnostics and software businesses to create a company focused on providing telehealth, the West Palm Beach, Fla. -based provider said last week.

- 문제가 생기면, 회사를 나누기도 한다.[5] vex 괴롭히다.

4) Rennova Health to spin off 2 units, create telehealth company Alia Paavola— Monday, June 15th, 2020. Becker's Hospital Review
5) How Companies Spin Off Environmental Liabilities to Avoid Legal Obligations BY DAVID F. LARCKER, ANDREW BAKER, BRIAN TAYAN November 25, 2020 promarket.org

- 형태 form → figure[fígjər]. figure out = 알아내다.

Environmental externalities are vexing for corporate decision makers, but some companies have figured out a way to deal with them: a spinoff. A recent case study explores a troubling practice of companies attempting to separate themselves from environmental liability through the spinoff of thinly capitalized subsidiaries.

- 드라마나 영화도 spin-off가 있다.

"Creed" is the greatest spin-off of all time.

- spin-off 경우, 원작이 덜 중요하다. 사건, 인물, 주제에 더 초점을 맞춘다. 1976년 록키 Rocky 원작의 존재감은, 영화 Creed에서는 떨어진다.
- 후속편 sequel[síːkwəl] 경우에는 원작을 충실히 '따른다 follow.' 1979년 <록키2>, 1981년 <록키3>, 1985년 <록키4>, 1990년 <록키5>, 2006년 <록키 발보아>
- 따라가는 순서 = sequence[síːkwəns]
- 따라가는 결과 = consequence[kɑ́nsəkwèns]
- spin out도 있다. 자동차가 균형을 잃고 도는 것이다.
- slide[slaid]-slid-slid[slid]이다.

My car spun out in the snow and slid off the road.

■ 이해하기 혼란스럽지만, 분사하다 역시 spin out.[6]

In an effort to simplify the IoT world, Deutsche
Telekom is spinning out its Internet of Things unit
and launching what it calls the "world's first open
platform" for IoT.

■ 회사가 떨어져 나가다 → 떨어져 나간 회사

spin out → spinoff, spin-off
spin off → spinoff, spin-off

---

6) Ray Le Maistre. Telecom TV. 2020.6.20. Deutsche Telekom to
spin out IoT unit, launch global open 'hub'

16 carry, move, convey, haul

- carry = 가지고 다니다. move = ~의 위치를 옮기다.
- 임신한 아이를 가지다 = carry[kǽri]

A baby is something you carry for nine months, in your arms for three years, and in your heart until the day you die.

- miscarry = 유산하다 <아이를 가지고 다니지 않게 되다>

---

mis(not) + carry = miscarry

- 유산 = miscarriage[miskǽridʒ]. 태아 fetus[fíːtəs].

A miscarriage is an event that results in the loss of a fetus before 20 weeks of pregnancy.

I miscarried a baby ten years ago.

- prayer[prɛər] 기도. faith[feiθ] 신념.

Prayer is asking for rain and faith is carrying the umbrella. - Barbara Johnson

- carry 대신 move[muːv]를 넣으면, 뜻이 전혀 달라진다.
- Move the umbrella! = 그 우산이 있는 위치를 바꾸어라! 여기서 위치는 우산이 향하는 각도도 포함된다.
- move = 위치를 옮기다.
- dare 감히 ~하다, 용기. chessmen 체스 말(복수형).

Daring ideas are like chessmen moved forward. They may be beaten, but they may start a winning game. - Johann Wolfgang von Goethe

Move out of your comfort zone. You can only grow if you are willing to feel awkward and uncomfortable when you try something new. - Brian Tracy

- move = 마음이 움직이다.
- It moved me to tears! = 마음이 움직여 눈물이 났다!

Great journalism will always attract readers. The

words, pictures and graphics that are the stuff of journalism have to be brilliantly packaged: they must feed the mind and move the heart. - Rupert Murdoch

Japan is the most intoxicating place for me. In Kyoto, there's an inn called the Tawaraya which is quite extraordinary. The Japanese culture fascinates me: the food, the dress, the manners and the traditions. It's the travel experience that has moved me the most. - Roman Coppola

- enormous[inɔ́ːrməs] = e<out of> + normous<norm>

It moved me enormously. I kept thinking about the terrible things that man was able to do to other men - and keeps on doing. - Marc Ash

- it moved me = 감동을 주었다. it moved me … to a bigger house! = 나를 더 큰 집으로 옮기게 해줬다.

How can you vote for Burns's movie? Let's just say it moved me … to a bigger house! - The Simpons

- convey[kənvéi] = 여기서 저기로 옮기다
- essential[isénʃəl] 없애거나 뺄 수 없는. raise 위로 올리다. eyebrow[áibràu] 눈썹. message[mésidʒ] 전하는 말.

Do whatever it takes to convey your essential self.
- Martha Beck

You can convey a lot of emotion with just some eyebrows and mouth movement. - Gillian Jacobs

If you want to convey a message, you must do so in an enjoyable format. - Sushmita Sen

Art is not journalism. In art, you don't make it to convey a message. - Pawel Pawlikowski

■ haul[hɔːl] = 무거운 것을 옮기다. 예로는 건축자재, 사람.

My wife and I hauled the construction materials ourselves.

We will never get to the flying car era. We will get to the era where we get flying drones that haul people, though. - Thomas Frey

It does seem really hard to get consumers to do the right thing. It is stupid that we use two tons of steel, glass, and plastic to haul our sorry selves to the shopping mall. - John Doerr

서양인의 삶과 영어 표현

17 인류의 공통점: 놀이와 도박

> ## back to square one 원점으로 돌아가다

- 첫 번째 정사각형 square[skwɛər] = square one. 보드게임 첫 칸으로 되돌아오면, 실망스러운 원점으로 온 것이다. 그림은 19세기 Snakes and Ladders 게임이다.[1]
- e<out> + vaporate<vapor> = evaporate[ivǽpərèit]

There are a lot of guys who are successful, they make a lot of big money, I mean millions overnight with a contract, and they don't understand the evaporation. It evaporates. You're always back to square one. I found that out, so integrity is how I do business. That's my main asset. - George Foreman

---

[1] https://commons.wikimedia.org/wiki/File:Snakes−and−ladders.png
Early Form of Snakes and Ladders game. Patented 1893.

There is no such thing as going back to square one. Remember that you are starting over with more knowledge, strength and power than you had before. Your journey was never over, it was just waiting for you to find it again. - Lori Deschene

■ 중립적 원점으로서 쓰이는 경우도 있다.

Most sitcoms and cartoons, especially, you can rely on, because they go back to square one at the beginning of every episode. - Scott Adsit

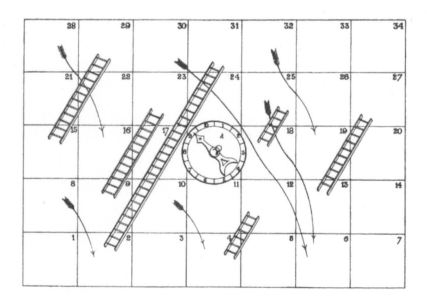

ace up one's sleeve = 속임수 혹은 숨겨둔 무기

- 트럼프 카드놀이에서 제일 높은 패는 에이스. 이런 좋은 패를 소매에 숨겨 두었다가 결정적 순간에 꺼내 든다. 속임수나 비장의 무엇을 의미한다.
- 여기서 up은 위쪽이라는 위치를 나타낸다. 소매 위 쪽 = up one's sleeve.
- 놀라운 카드, 롬멜은 비행기 잡는 포를 탱크 파괴에 쓴다.

She has several tricks up her sleeve.

He has a few cards up his sleeve.

In Africa, Erwin Rommel had an ace up his sleeve: 88mm anti-aircraft gun.

18 일상으로서 예술과 공연

---

usher in = ~을 시작하다

■ usher[ˈʌʃə(r)] = 공연장에서 자리를 안내해주는 사람, 자리를 안내해주다.

■ usher 이 사람이 중요하다. 문을 열어주고 안으로 into 들여보내 주어야, 안에 in 있을 수 있다. into → in. 그래

야 공연을 볼 수 있다.

- usher in = (시대를) 시작하다, (새로운 무엇을) 시작하다.
- 열어 준다! 19세기 네덜란드 미술 황금시대! usher은?
- 빈센트 반 고흐, 조르주 브레이트너, 안톤 마우베!

The late 19th century however, formed a 'Second Golden Age.' Artists like Vincent van Gogh, George Breitner and Anton Mauve ushered in a whole new era of art.

The '90s will be looked back on as ushering in an era of comfort. - Michael Kors

Be glad today. Tomorrow may bring tears. Be brave today. The darkest night will pass. And golden rays will usher in the dawn. - Sarah Knowles Bolton

Sin will usher in the greatest and the saddest losses that can be upon our souls. - Thomas Brooks

It is not the simple statement of facts that ushers in freedom; it is the constant repetition of them that has this liberating effect. Tolerance is the result not of enlightenment, but of boredom. - Quentin Crisp

> ## walk a tightrope = 조금만 실수하면 큰일나게 생기다

- 그림은 줄을 타는 사람의 불안한 상황을 잘 묘사한다.[1] 이 그림처럼, 조금만 잘못된 판단을 하거나 행동을 하면 끔찍한 결과가 생기는 경우이다.
- 팽팽한 tight 밧줄 rope → tightrope 곡예사가 쓰는 줄

Acting is the most insecure profession in the world - you're insecure if you're successful, you're insecure if you're not. A tightrope walk without a net. It's a miracle I'm still standing! - Kabir Bedi

Many manufacturers have to walk a tightrope between pricing their goods too high and not selling them, and pricing them low and losing money.[2]

---

1) https://ac-illust.com/ko/clip-art/876768/
2) Cambridge Dictionary

19 서양인 삶에서의 항해

> **learn the ropes = 일을 배우다**

- 그림은 배 위에서 줄을 다루는 것이 무엇인지 잘 보여준다.[1] 일을 배운다는 뜻이다.

- sub\<under\> + stitute\<put\> = 대체하다[sʌbstətjùːt]
- substitute 동사와 명사 모두 다, 첫 모음에 강세가 있다.

---

1) https://ac-illust.com/ko/clip-art/2026887/

- substitute = 대체품. substitution = 대체
- 설탕은 꿀로 대체할 수 있다.
  - = You can substitute honey for sugar.
  - = Honey can be substituted for sugar.
  - = Honey is a sugar substitute.

Generally, if you're a baker who's still learning the ropes, substitutions can be risky. It's always best to make a recipe the first time as written, and only after that initial success should you make substitutions. - Claire Saffitz

Learning how to interact with customers is something that anyone starting any business must master. It's an amazing opportunity to be able to learn the ropes at an established company and then employ your expertise at your own company. - Marc Benioff

We learn the rope of life by untying its knots. - Jean Toomer

---

rock the boat = 문제를 일으키다

- 글자 그대로 굳이 이해를 하자면, 배를 앞뒤로 흔들어 난파시키는 행위이다.
- 이러한 의미로는 쓰이지 않는다. 배와는 전혀 상관없는 맥

락으로 사용한다.

- 문제를 일으킨다는 의미이다. 따지거나 싸움을 걸거나 해서 이런 저런 불편한 상황이 벌어진다는 부정적 느낌이다.
- 하지만 이 표현은 점점 덜 부정적이 되어가고 있다.
- 다음 인용문에서 그런 것을 느낄 수 있다. 점점 더 긍정적으로 쓰인다.
- 이제 사람들이 삐딱함을 더 긍정적으로 보는 것일까?

- row[rou] = 노를 젓다
- race[reis] = 인종
- vogue[voug] = 유행. 여기서는 잡지 이름이다.

The man who rows the boat seldom has time to rock it. - Bill Copeland

Only the guy who isn't rowing has time to rock the boat. - Jean-Paul Sartre

I've always been quite scared about talking about race. You don't wanna rock the boat because you want to keep working. - Wunmi Mosaku

I feel it would be a huge mistake for 'Vogue' always to be completely tasteful, completely perfect. I think it's very important for us to also rock the boat. - Anna Wintour

---

pass with flying colors = 독보적 성과를 내다

- 대항해 시대에 범선이 깃발 flag을 돛대 높은 곳에 달고서 배가 지나가면 pass, 승리를 거두고 돌아오는 것이다.
- 한데 당시 영국에서는 '깃발 flag'을 'colour'이라고 불렀

다. 영국식 영어라서, colour.

■ pass with flying colors, 말 그대로 의미는 나부끼는 깃
발을 달고 지나가다. fly[flai] = 깃발이나 연이 나부끼다

■ pass with flying colors = pass with flying colours =
시험, 경쟁, 평가 등에서 독보적인 성과를 내다

■ hang in there 표현은, 권투에서 나왔다. 줄에 매달려! 코
치가 힘들어하는 선수에게 외치는 말이다.

Life is a HUGE test … if you hang in there through
bullshit, you will pass with flying colors!

When you really want something, sometimes you
have to swim a little deeper. You can't give up just
because things don't come easy. You have to
overcome the obstacles and face your fears. But in
the end, it's all worthwhile. Life is full of ups and
down, but if you believe in yourself, you will
always come through with flying colors. Value
friendship, love and faith. Never underestimate
yourself. Believe in yourself! HAVE A GOOD LIFE!

부록

앞에 붙는 어원(출처: Webster's, Cambridge, Oxford)

a (without)
abyss <w/o + bottom> anesthesia <w/o + sensation> anonymous <w/o + name> apathy <w/o + feeling>

ab (off, apart, away from)
abhor <from + horror> abdicate <off + proclaim> abject <away from + throw> absent <away from + be>

ad (to, toward)
acclaim <to + cry out> adapt <to + fit> adequate <to + equal> admit <to + send> adopt <to + choose> adventure <to + come> advocate <to + call> affect <to + do> aggravate <to + heavy> alleviate <to + light> announce <to + messenger> appetite <to + desire> appeal <to + drive> apply <to + fold> assess <to + sit>

com (with, together)
commute <w + change> companion <w + bread> compel <w + drive> complete <w + fill> compose <w + place> compromise <w + promise> concentrate <w + center> conceive <w + take> concur <w + run> conclude <w + close> congregate <w + gathering> congress <w + walk> consent <w + feel, sense> conserve <w + keep> construct <w + pile> constitute <w + set>

de (down)
decline <down + bend> deposit <down + put> descend <down + climb> devalue <down + value>

ex (out, out of)
eccentric <out of + center> effect <out + do> excavate <out + hollow> exceed <out + go> excel <out + rise> except <out + take> exclude <out + close> exempt <out + buy> exhibit <out + hold> expand <out + spread> expect <out + look> expel <out + drive>

im, in (in, into)
incise <into + cut> include<in + close> incur <in + run> indicate <in + declare> implement <in + fill> improve <in + gain> imply <in + fold> influence <in + flow> institute <in + set> influx <in + flow>

in (not)
insane <not + healthy> incompetent <not + compete>

ob (against, opposite)
obstacle <against + stand> obstruct <against + pile up> offend <against + hit> oppose <against + place>

ob (towards, in the direction of)
obey <towards + hear> oblige <toward + bind>

per (through, throughout)
perceive <t/o + take> permanent <t/o + remain> permit <t/o + send> pervert <t/o + turn>

pre (before)

precede <before + move> precise <before + cut>

pro (forth, forward)

proceed <fw + go> procrastinate <fw + tomorrow> profound <fw + bottom> progress <fw + step> prolong <fw + long> propel <fw + drive> propose <fw + place>

re (back, again)

receive <back + take> recluse <back + shut, close> recruit <again + grow> recur <back + run> redeem <back + get> regress <back + go> repel <back + drive> replete <back + fill> reply <back + fold> resent <again + sense> reserve <back + keep> respect <back + look at> review <again + see> revive <again + live>

se (apart)

secede <apart + go> seclude <apart + close> segregate <apart + gathering> separate <apart + arrange>

sub (under)

supply <under + fill> suppose <under + put>

sur (beyond, above, over)

surpass <beyond + pass> survive <above + live>

trans (across, over, beyond)

transcend <over + climb> transient <over + go>

저자약력

김준우

미시간주립대 사회학-도시학 박사
싱가포르국립대 박사후과정
부산발전연구원 부연구위원
전남대 사회학과 교수

저역서
『사회과학의 현대통계학』(김영채 공저) 박영사
『즐거운 SPSS, 풀리는 통계학』박영사
『국가와 도시』전남대학교출판부 2008년 문화체육관광부 선정 우수학술도서
『선집으로 읽는 한국의 도시와 지역』(안영진 공편) 박영사
『공간이론과 한국도시의 현실』전남대학교출판부
『황금도시: 장소의 정치경제학』전남대학교출판부
John R. Logan & Harvey L. Molotch(2007), *Urban Fortunes: The Political Economy of Place*, The University of California.
『새로운 지역격차와 새로운 처방: 철근/콘크리트에서 지역발전유발 지식서비스로』(안영진 공저) 박영사
『서울권의 등장과 나머지의 쇠퇴』전남대학교출판부
『미국이라는 공간: 부동산 투기·노예제·인종 차별·인디언 제거·뺏기는 삶의 터전』박영사

어원 + 어원 = 영단어

초판발행	2021년 3월 10일
지은이	김준우
펴낸이	안종만 · 안상준
편 집	우석진
기획/마케팅	이후근
표지디자인	최윤주
제 작	고철민 · 조영환
펴낸곳	(주) **박영사**
	서울특별시 금천구 가산디지털2로 53, 210호(가산동, 한라시그마밸리)
	등록 1959. 3. 11. 제300-1959-1호(倫)
전 화	02)733-6771
f a x	02)736-4818
e-mail	pys@pybook.co.kr
homepage	www.pybook.co.kr
ISBN	979-11-303-1211-8 93740

copyright©김준우, 2021, Printed in Korea

정 가   7,000원